BEST FOOD fast

THE AUSTRALIAN Women's Weekly

An hour or less to get dinner on the table? Now where was that quick-and-easy stir-fry I saw in my copy of *The Australian Women's Weekly* magazine? Sound familiar? Well, there's now no need to look any further. Here are all your favourite fast and simple recipes from your most-loved magazine. We've also thrown in a few speedy starters and desserts, leaving you more time to do the things you love most ... which in my case is reading the rest of the latest issue of the *Women's Weekly* magazine!

Pamela Clark

Food Director

contents

STARTERS

PREPARATION TIME
10 MINS
(PLUS STANDING TIME)

COOKING TIME
15 MINS

chicken sang choy bow

4 dried shiitake mushrooms

1 tablespoon peanut oil

1kg chicken mince

4cm piece fresh ginger (20g), chopped finely

1 clove garlic, crushed

227g can water chestnuts, drained, chopped coarsely

227g can sliced bamboo shoots, drained, chopped coarsely

¼ cup (60ml) hoisin sauce

¼ cup (60ml) oyster sauce

2 tablespoons soy sauce

2 tablespoons cornflour

½ cup (125ml) chicken stock

3 cups (240g) bean sprouts

4 green onions, sliced thickly

18 large butter lettuce leaves

You need about two medium butter lettuce for this recipe.

1 Place mushrooms in small heatproof bowl, cover with boiling water; stand 20 minutes, drain. Discard stems; chop mushroom caps finely.
2 Heat oil in wok; stir-fry chicken, ginger and garlic until chicken is just changed in colour.
3 Add mushrooms with water chestnuts, bamboo shoots, sauces and blended cornflour and stock; stir-fry until mixture boils and thickens. Stir in sprouts and onion.
4 Divide lettuce leaves among serving plates; spoon sang choy bow into lettuce leaves.

serves 6
per serving 17.7g total fat (4.7g saturated fat); 1513kJ (362 cal); 15.4g carbohydrate; 35.4g protein; 4.6g fibre

chicken skewers with chilli and lime sauce

⅓ cup (80ml) sweet chilli sauce

2 tablespoons fish sauce

2 tablespoons lime juice

6 chicken thigh fillets (660g), halved lengthways

1 green onion, sliced thinly

You need to soak 12 bamboo skewers in water for a least 30 minutes before use to prevent splintering and scorching.

1 Combine sauces and juice in small bowl; reserve half of the sauce in small serving bowl.
2 Thread chicken onto skewers lengthways; brush chicken with remaining sauce. Cook skewers on heated oiled grill plate (or grill or barbecue) until cooked through.
3 Add onion to reserved sauce; serve sauce with skewers.

TIP Uncooked skewers are suitable to freeze.

serves 4
per serving 12.1g total fat (3.6g saturated fat); 1108kJ (265 cal); 7.3g carbohydrate; 31.6g protein; 0.2g fibre

PREPARATION TIME
25 MINS
COOKING TIME
15 MINS

pork dumplings

1 Using hand, combine pork, cabbage, onion, chives, ginger, sauce and cornflour in medium bowl.
2 Place 1 level teaspoon of the pork mixture into centre of each wonton wrapper; brush edges with a little water, pinch edges together to seal.
3 Place dumplings, in batches, in large bamboo steamer. Set over large saucepan of boiling water; cover, steam about 4 minutes or until cooked through. Remove with slotted spoon; drain well.
4 Meanwhile, combine dipping sauce ingredients in small bowl.
5 Serve dumplings with dipping sauce.

makes 40
per dumpling 0.6g total fat (0.2g saturated fat); 113kJ (27 cal); 3.5g carbohydrate; 1.9g protein; 0.2g fibre

250g pork mince

½ cup (40g) finely chopped chinese cabbage

2 green onions, chopped finely

2 tablespoons finely chopped fresh garlic chives

2cm piece fresh ginger (10g), grated

2 teaspoons soy sauce

2 teaspoons cornflour

40 wonton wrappers

DIPPING SAUCE

¼ cup (60ml) soy sauce

2 teaspoons white vinegar

2 teaspoons brown sugar

moroccan lamb cutlets

1 teaspoon ground coriander

2 teaspoons ground cumin

2 teaspoons sweet paprika

¼ teaspoon cayenne pepper

1 clove garlic, crushed

1 tablespoon finely chopped fresh flat-leaf parsley

2 tablespoons olive oil

24 french-trimmed lamb cutlets (960g)

1 teaspoon cumin seeds, toasted

¼ cup (60g) prepared baba ghanoush

Prepared baba ghanoush can be purchased from some supermarkets and delicatessens.

1 Combine ground coriander, ground cumin, sweet paprika, cayenne pepper, garlic, parsley and oil in medium bowl; rub mixture all over lamb.
2 Cook lamb on heated oiled grill plate (or grill or barbecue) until cooked as desired.
3 Sprinkle lamb with cumin seeds; serve lamb with baba ghanoush.

serves 6
per serving 14.8g total fat (4.7g saturated fat); 974kJ (233 cal); 0.5g carbohydrate; 24.5g protein; 1.1g fibre

croûtes with goats cheese and rocket salad

4 thick slices white bread (180g)

2 tablespoons olive oil

1 clove garlic, crushed

4 slices prosciutto (60g)

50g baby rocket leaves

2 tablespoons balsamic vinegar

2 tablespoons olive oil, extra

80g goats cheese, cut into four slices

1 Preheat grill.
2 Using 9cm cutter, cut one round from each bread slice. Brush both sides of bread with combined oil and garlic; toast bread both sides.
3 Grill prosciutto until crisp.
4 Divide rocket among serving plates; drizzle with combined vinegar and extra oil, top with croûtes, cheese then prosciutto.

serves 4
per serving 23.5g total fat (5.2g saturated fat); 1388kJ (332 cal); 20.8g carbohydrate; 9.5g protein; 1.6g fibre

PREPARATION TIME
10 MINS
COOKING TIME
5 MINS

gazpacho

1 Blend or process half of the cucumber and half of the capsicum with remaining ingredients until just smooth.
2 Push vegetable mixture through sieve or food mill into large jug.
3 Serve gazpacho in glasses topped with remaining cucumber and remaining capsicum.

serves 4
per serving 14g total fat (1.9g saturated fat); 790kJ (189 cal); 12.5g carbohydrate; 3.3g protein; 2.7g fibre

1 lebanese cucumber (130g), peeled, seeded, chopped finely

1 medium green capsicum (200g), chopped finely

1 litre (4 cups) chilled vegetable juice

¼ cup (60ml) olive oil

2 cloves garlic, crushed

1 tablespoon red wine vinegar

1 tablespoon tomato paste

1 teaspoon white sugar

¼ teaspoon Tabasco sauce

[PREPARATION TIME
15 MINS]

smoked salmon with avocado salsa and prawns

24 slices smoked salmon (400g)

16 cooked medium king prawns (720g)

1 tablespoon salmon roe

8 fresh dill sprigs

AVOCADO SALSA

2 medium egg tomatoes (150g), seeded, chopped finely

2 small avocados (400g), chopped finely

½ small red onion (50g), chopped finely

1 tablespoon finely chopped fresh chives

2 teaspoons finely chopped fresh dill

1 teaspoon finely grated lemon rind

2 tablespoons lemon juice

LEMON CHIVE DRESSING

¼ cup (60ml) olive oil

2 tablespoons lemon juice

1 tablespoon finely chopped fresh chives

1 Combine avocado salsa ingredients in small bowl.
2 Line eight holes of a 12-hole (⅓-cup/80ml) muffin pan with plastic wrap, bringing the plastic 3cm above the edge of the holes. Place one salmon slice in base of each hole and fold over excess. Top each slice with 2 tablespoons of the salsa; lay another slice of salmon in each hole. Top each with another 2 tablespoons of the salsa; lay another slice of salmon in each hole. Fold over plastic to seal; refrigerate until required.
3 Shell and devein prawns, leaving tails intact.
4 Place lemon chive dressing ingredients in screw-top jar; shake well.
5 Turn out and unwrap salmon parcels. Divide parcels among serving plates; top with prawns, roe and dill, drizzle with dressing.

makes 8
per parcel 17.7g total fat (3.3g saturated fat); 1083kJ (259 cal); 1.1g carbohydrate; 23.7g protein; 0.9g fibre

olive and tomato bruschetta

1 loaf ciabatta (440g)

⅓ cup (80ml) extra virgin olive oil

1 cup (150g) seeded kalamata olives, chopped coarsely

1 cup (150g) stuffed green olives, chopped coarsely

1 cup (150g) coarsely chopped drained sun-dried tomatoes

1 tablespoon baby capers, rinsed, drained

2 anchovy fillets, drained, chopped finely

¼ cup finely shredded fresh basil

1 clove garlic, crushed

2 tablespoons red wine vinegar

1 Preheat grill.
2 Cut bread into 1.5cm slices; brush with ¼ cup of the oil. Toast bread both sides.
3 Meanwhile, combine remaining oil and remaining ingredients in medium bowl.
4 Place bread on serving plates; top with olive mixture.

TIP Olive mixture can be made a day ahead and kept, covered, in refrigerator.

makes 20
per bruschetta 5.5g total fat (0.8g saturated fat); 497kJ (119 cal); 14.3g carbohydrate; 2.9g protein; 2.4g fibre

[PREPARATION TIME
10 MINS]

oysters with lime and coriander

1 Carefully remove oysters from shells. Wash and dry shells; return oysters to shells.
2 Place remaining ingredients in screw-top jar; shake well. Divide dressing among oysters.

TIP Dressing can be made a day ahead.

makes 24
per oyster 1g total fat (0.2g saturated fat); 67kJ (16 cal); 0.3g carbohydrate; 1.3g protein; 0.1g fibre

24 oysters, on the half shell

¼ cup (60ml) lime juice

1 teaspoon Tabasco sauce

2 tablespoons coarsely chopped fresh coriander

2 green onions, sliced thinly

1 tablespoon peanut oil

1 clove garlic, crushed

1 teaspoon brown sugar

steamed mussels with saffron, chilli and coriander

¾ cup (180ml) dry white wine

¼ teaspoon saffron threads

1 tablespoon fish sauce

2 teaspoons finely grated lime rind

2kg medium black mussels

1 tablespoon peanut oil

5cm piece fresh ginger (25g), grated coarsely

2 cloves garlic, crushed

3 fresh small red thai chillies, sliced thinly

½ cup loosely packed fresh coriander leaves

1 Bring wine to a boil in small saucepan. Stir in saffron, sauce and rind; remove from heat. Stand 10 minutes.

2 Meanwhile, scrub mussels; remove beards.

3 Heat oil in large saucepan; cook ginger, garlic and chilli, stirring, until fragrant. Add wine mixture and mussels; bring to a boil. Reduce heat; simmer, covered, about 5 minutes or until mussels open (discard any that do not).

4 Spoon mussels and broth into serving bowls; sprinkle with coriander.

serves 6
per serving 1.3g total fat (0.9g saturated fat); 451kJ (108 cal); 3.8g carbohydrate; 8.4g protein; 0.6g fibre

tom yum goong

16 uncooked medium king prawns (720g)

1 tablespoon peanut oil

10cm stick (20g) finely chopped fresh lemon grass

2 cloves garlic, crushed

4cm piece fresh ginger (20g), grated coarsely

3 cups (750ml) water

1.125 litres (4½ cups) fish stock

3 fresh small red thai chillies, sliced thinly

2 fresh kaffir lime leaves, shredded finely

¼ cup (60ml) fish sauce

⅓ cup (80ml) lime juice

4 green onions, sliced thinly

¼ cup loosely packed fresh coriander leaves

¼ cup loosely packed fresh thai basil leaves

1 Shell and devein prawns, leaving tails intact; reserve prawn heads and shells.

2 Heat oil in large saucepan; cook prawn shells and heads, stirring, about 3 minutes or until shells and heads are deep orange in colour. Add lemon grass, garlic and ginger; cook, stirring, until fragrant.

3 Stir in the water, stock, chilli and lime leaves; bring to a boil. Reduce heat; simmer, uncovered, 10 minutes. Strain stock through muslin-lined sieve into large heatproof bowl; discard solids.

4 Return stock to same cleaned pan; bring to a boil. Add prawns, reduce heat; simmer, uncovered, until prawns are changed in colour. Remove from heat; stir in sauce and juice. Serve soup sprinkled with onion and herbs.

serves 4
per serving 5.9g total fat (1g saturated fat); 686kJ (164 cal); 3.6g carbohydrate; 23.2g protein; 1.1g fibre

PREPARATION TIME
15 MINS
COOKING TIME
20 MINS

chilli salt squid

1 Gently separate bodies and tentacles of squid by pulling on tentacles. Cut head from tentacles just below eyes; discard head. Trim long tentacle of each squid; remove the clear quill from inside body.

2 Peel inside flaps from squid with salted fingers, then peel away dark skin. Wash squid well and pat dry with absorbent paper.

3 Cut along one side of the squid and open out; score inside surface in diagonal pattern. Cut squid in half lengthways; cut each half in half crossways.

4 Heat oil in wok; deep-fry sliced chilli until soft. Remove from wok; drain on absorbent paper. Deep-fry coriander for a few seconds or until changed in colour. Remove from wok; drain on absorbent paper.

5 Combine flour, chopped chilli, salt and pepper in medium bowl. Toss squid in flour mixture; shake away excess. Deep-fry squid, in batches, until just browned and tender; drain on absorbent paper. Serve squid sprinkled with sliced chilli and coriander.

TIP Take care when deep-frying the chillies and coriander, as the oil may spit.

serves 6
per serving 6g total fat (0.9g saturated fat); 610kJ (146 cal); 9.1g carbohydrate; 13.6g protein; 1g fibre

1kg small whole squid

vegetable oil, for deep-frying

2 fresh long red chillies, sliced thinly

1 cup loosely packed fresh coriander leaves

½ cup (75g) plain flour

2 fresh long red chillies, chopped finely

2 teaspoons sea salt flakes

1 teaspoon cracked black pepper

PREPARATION TIME
30 MINS
COOKING TIME
10 MINS

SALADS + SIDES

[
PREPARATION TIME
10 MINS
COOKING TIME
20 MINS
]

grilled radicchio and roasted tomato salad

⅓ cup (80ml) olive oil

1 clove garlic, crushed

6 medium egg tomatoes (450g), halved

4 small radicchio (600g), quartered

2 tablespoons balsamic vinegar

100g baby rocket leaves

⅔ cup (50g) shaved pecorino cheese

1 Preheat oven to hot.
2 Combine 1 tablespoon of the oil with garlic in small bowl. Place tomato, cut-side up, on oven tray; drizzle with oil mixture. Roast, uncovered, in hot oven about 20 minutes or until softened.
3 Meanwhile, combine radicchio with 2 tablespoons of the remaining oil in large bowl. Cook radicchio on heated oiled grill plate (or grill or barbecue) until browned all over; cool 5 minutes.
4 Place vinegar and remaining oil in screw-top jar; shake well. Arrange tomato, radicchio and rocket on large serving platter; sprinkle with cheese, drizzle with dressing.

serves 6
per serving 14.9g total fat (3.2g saturated fat); 681kJ (163 cal); 2.9g carbohydrate; 4.6g protein; 3g fibre

table

preparation

PREPARATION TIME
10 MINS
COOKING TIME
15 MINS

mustard and sweet onion mash

1kg potatoes, diced into
3cm pieces

1 tablespoon olive oil

80g butter

2 large brown onions (400g),
sliced thinly

2 teaspoons brown sugar

2 teaspoons balsamic vinegar

½ cup (125ml) milk, warmed

1 tablespoon dijon mustard

*We used nicola potatoes, but there are many other varieties,
such as lasoda, pink-eye or sebago, suitable for mashing.*

1 Boil, steam or microwave potato until tender; drain.
2 Meanwhile, heat oil and 20g of the butter in large frying pan; cook
   onion, stirring, over low heat, about 15 minutes or until onion browns
   lightly. Add sugar and vinegar; cook, stirring, until sugar dissolves.
3 Mash potato in medium bowl with milk and remaining butter until
   smooth. Stir mustard and half of the onion mixture into mash.
4 Serve mash topped with remaining onion mixture.

serves 4
per serving 22.6g total fat (12.3g saturated fat); 1568kJ (375 cal);
35.2g carbohydrate; 7.8g protein; 4.8g fibre

PREPARATION TIME
[15 MINS]

smoked chicken and pear salad

1 Place red wine vinaigrette ingredients in screw-top jar; shake well.
2 Place ingredients and vinaigrette in large bowl; toss to combine.

serves 4
per serving 16.2g total fat (2.6g saturated fat); 957kJ (229 cal); 11.2g carbohydrate; 9.6g protein; 3.8g fibre

1 small radicchio (100g), torn

1 small mignonette lettuce, torn

200g smoked chicken, sliced thinly

1 large pear (330g), sliced thinly

1 medium red onion (170g), sliced thinly

RED WINE VINAIGRETTE

¼ cup (60ml) red wine vinegar

2 tablespoons balsamic vinegar

¼ cup (60ml) olive oil

moroccan beef salad

1 cup (250ml) vegetable stock

1½ cups (300g) couscous

½ cup (75g) thinly sliced
dried apricots

½ cup (80g) sultanas

1 medium red onion (170g),
chopped finely

¼ cup finely chopped fresh mint

2 tablespoons coarsely chopped
fresh dill

600g beef rump steak

1 tablespoon toasted pine nuts

2 teaspoons cumin seeds

¾ cup (180ml) oil-free
french dressing

1 Bring stock to a boil in medium saucepan; remove from heat. Add couscous to stock, cover; stand about 5 minutes or until stock is absorbed, fluffing with fork occasionally. Transfer couscous to large bowl; stir in apricots, sultanas, onion and herbs.

2 Meanwhile, cook beef in heated oiled frying pan until cooked as desired. Cover beef; stand 5 minutes. Slice thinly.

3 Place nuts and seeds in small heated frying pan; cook, stirring, until fragrant and nuts are toasted. Place nut mixture in screw-top jar with dressing; shake well.

4 Serve beef on couscous mixture; drizzle with dressing.

serves 4
per serving 13.5g total fat (4.9g saturated fat); 2834kJ (678 cal); 91.5g carbohydrate; 46.5g protein; 4.4g fibre

lamb and red lentil salad

1 cup (200g) red lentils

600g lamb backstraps

3 medium tomatoes (450g), chopped coarsely

1 trimmed celery stick (100g), chopped finely

6 green onions, chopped finely

¼ cup loosely packed fresh coriander leaves

50g rocket leaves

CUMIN DRESSING

⅓ cup (80ml) lemon juice

2 tablespoons olive oil

1 teaspoon ground cumin

1 teaspoon sweet paprika

1 Rinse lentils under cold water; drain. Place lentils in medium saucepan, cover with cold water; bring to a boil. Reduce heat; simmer, uncovered, about 5 minutes or until just tender, drain. Rinse under cold water; drain.

2 Cook lamb on heated oiled grill plate (or grill or barbecue) until cooked as desired.

3 Meanwhile, place ingredients for cumin dressing in screw-top jar; shake well.

4 Place lentils in large bowl with tomato, celery, onion, coriander and dressing; toss gently to combine.

5 Serve lamb with lentil salad and rocket.

serves 4
per serving 23.6g total fat (7.4g saturated fat); 2015kJ (482 cal); 22.9g carbohydrate; 45.4g protein; 9.2g fibre

PREPARATION TIME
10 MINS
COOKING TIME
15 MINS

warm salmon, risoni and pea salad

1 Cook pasta in large saucepan of boiling water, uncovered, until almost tender. Add peas to pan with pasta and cook until peas and pasta are just tender; drain.
2 Meanwhile, place dill dressing ingredients in screw-top jar; shake well.
3 Heat oil in large frying pan; cook fish, uncovered, until cooked as desired. Remove from pan; stand 5 minutes. Discard skin and any bones. Flake fish into large chunks.
4 Place pasta, peas and fish in large bowl with onion, spinach and dressing; toss gently to combine.

serves 4
per serving 23.6g total fat (4.1g saturated fat); 2324kJ (556 cal); 49g carbohydrate; 3.6g protein; 7.8g fibre

250g risoni

2 cups (240g) frozen peas

1 tablespoon olive oil

500g salmon fillets

8 green onions, sliced thickly

100g baby spinach leaves

DILL DRESSING

2 tablespoons olive oil

2 teaspoons finely grated lemon rind

¼ cup (60ml) lemon juice

1 teaspoon dijon mustard

1 tablespoon coarsely chopped fresh dill

PREPARATION TIME
15 MINS
COOKING TIME
10 MINS

vegetable, bean and basil salad

Many varieties of already cooked white beans are available canned, among them cannellini, butter and haricot beans; any of these is suitable for this salad.

340g asparagus, trimmed, cut into 4cm lengths

150g snow peas, trimmed, halved diagonally

1 small red oak leaf lettuce, torn

400g can white beans, rinsed, drained

250g cherry tomatoes, halved

200g fetta cheese, crumbled

1 cup loosely packed baby basil leaves

BASIL DRESSING

2 tablespoons finely chopped fresh basil

¼ cup (60ml) olive oil

2 tablespoons white wine vinegar

1 tablespoon lemon juice

1 teaspoon dijon mustard

1 Boil, steam or microwave asparagus and snow peas, separately, until just tender; drain. Rinse under cold water; drain.

2 Meanwhile, place basil dressing ingredients in screw-top jar; shake well.

3 Arrange lettuce on platter; top with asparagus, snow peas and beans, drizzle with a quarter of the dressing. Arrange tomato, cheese and basil on top; drizzle with remaining dressing.

serves 6
per serving 17.2g total fat (6.4g saturated fat); 878kJ (210 cal); 4.3g carbohydrate; 9.5g protein; 3.7g fibre

baby spinach and haloumi salad

340g asparagus, trimmed, cut into 5cm lengths

250g haloumi, sliced thinly

2 large avocados (640g), sliced thinly

200g baby spinach leaves

4 green onions, sliced thinly

CHIVE DRESSING

¼ cup (60ml) olive oil

2 tablespoons lemon juice

2 teaspoons finely chopped fresh chives

1 Boil, steam or microwave asparagus until tender; drain. Rinse under cold water; drain.

2 Meanwhile, place chive dressing ingredients in screw-top jar; shake well.

3 Heat large oiled non-stick frying pan; cook cheese, in batches, until browned lightly both sides.

4 Place asparagus and cheese in large bowl with remaining ingredients and dressing; toss gently to combine.

serves 4
per serving 49.9g total fat (14.3g saturated fat); 2207kJ (528 cal); 3.2g carbohydrate; 17.9g protein; 3.9g fibre

PREPARATION TIME
10 MINS
COOKING TIME
10 MINS

ham and asparagus spears with rocket salad

1 Wrap a piece of ham around two asparagus spears; secure with toothpicks. Repeat with remaining ham and asparagus. Cook on heated oiled grill plate (or grill or barbecue) until browned.
2 Meanwhile, divide rocket, tomato and basil among serving plates. Place vinegar and oil in screw-top jar; shake well.
3 Drizzle vegetables with dressing; top with cheese. Discard toothpicks; serve asparagus with salad.

serves 4
per serving 13.3g total fat (3.1g saturated fat); 928kJ (222 cal); 9.1g carbohydrate; 16.4g protein; 2.6g fibre

240g thinly sliced ham, halved

400g asparagus, trimmed

125g rocket leaves

250g yellow teardrop tomatoes, halved

2 tablespoons fresh baby basil leaves

2 tablespoons balsamic vinegar

2 tablespoons olive oil

¼ cup (20g) flaked parmesan cheese

chilli lime chicken salad

2 cups (500ml) water

2 cups (500ml) chicken stock

4 single chicken breasts fillets (680g)

1 small red capsicum (150g), sliced thinly

4 trimmed red radishes (60g), sliced thinly

¼ small chinese cabbage (175g), shredded coarsely

3 green onions, sliced thinly

1 cup (80g) bean sprouts

½ cup loosely packed fresh coriander leaves

½ cup (75g) toasted salted peanuts

CHILLI LIME DRESSING

⅓ cup (80ml) lime juice

¼ cup (65g) grated palm sugar

2 fresh small red thai chillies, chopped finely

1 clove garlic, crushed

1 tablespoon fish sauce

¼ cup (60ml) peanut oil

1 Bring the water and stock to a boil in large frying pan. Add chicken, reduce heat; simmer, covered, about 10 minutes or until cooked through. Remove from heat; cool chicken in liquid 10 minutes. Slice chicken thinly.
2 Meanwhile, make chilli lime dressing.
3 Place remaining ingredients and half of the dressing in large bowl; toss gently to combine.
4 Divide salad among serving plates; top with chicken, drizzle with remaining dressing.

CHILLI LIME DRESSING Combine juice, sugar, chilli and garlic in small saucepan. Stir over low heat until sugar dissolves; cool 10 minutes. Whisk in sauce and oil.

serves 4
per serving 27.2g total fat (4.2g saturated fat); 2157kJ (516 cal); 21.5g carbohydrate; 47g protein; 4g fibre

roast pumpkin and goat cheese salad

1kg pumpkin, chopped finely

2 tablespoons olive oil

2 cloves garlic, sliced thinly

2 tablespoons finely chopped fresh sage

½ cup (70g) pecans, chopped coarsely

8 large radicchio leaves (120g)

200g goat cheese

2 tablespoons lemon juice

1 Preheat oven to hot.
2 Combine pumpkin and half of the oil on oven tray; roast, uncovered, in hot oven 10 minutes. Add garlic and sage; roast, uncovered, about 5 minutes or until pumpkin is tender. Stir in nuts.
3 Divide radicchio leaves among serving plates; divide pumpkin mixture among leaves, top with cheese. Drizzle with combined juice and remaining oil; top with fresh sage leaves, if desired.

serves 4
per serving 30.5g total fat (7.9g saturated fat); 1609kJ (385 cal); 15.2g carbohydrate; 13.1g protein; 4.7g fibre

[
PREPARATION TIME
15 MINS
COOKING TIME
15 MINS
]

warm potato and chorizo salad

1 Boil, steam or microwave potato until just tender; drain.
2 Meanwhile, heat large non-stick frying pan; cook chorizo until crisp, remove from pan.
3 Place potato in same pan; cook, stirring gently, until browned lightly. Remove from pan.
4 Place combined oil, vinegar and sugar in same pan; bring to a boil. Boil, uncovered, about 2 minutes or until dressing reduces slightly.
5 Combine potato and chorizo in large bowl with onion, spinach and tomato; drizzle with dressing.

serves 4
per serving 33.2g total fat (12.1g saturated fat); 2086kJ (499 cal); 28.3g carbohydrate; 20.8g protein; 7.3g fibre

600g baby new potatoes, halved

3 chorizo sausages (510g), sliced thinly

1 tablespoon olive oil

½ cup (125ml) balsamic vinegar

2 teaspoons white sugar

1 small red onion (100g), sliced thinly

200g baby spinach leaves

250g cherry tomatoes, halved

PREPARATION TIME
10 MINS
COOKING TIME
20 MINS

prawn and avocado salad with ginger dressing

1kg cooked medium king prawns

200g snow peas, trimmed, sliced thinly

1 bunch fresh chives, cut into 4cm lengths

100g baby spinach leaves

1 medium avocado (250g), sliced thickly

GINGER DRESSING

12cm piece fresh ginger (60g), grated

2 tablespoons olive oil

2 tablespoons lemon juice

1 teaspoon white sugar

1 Shell and devein prawns; cut prawns in half lengthways.
2 Make ginger dressing.
3 Place prawns in large bowl with snow peas, chives, spinach, avocado and dressing; toss gently to combine.

GINGER DRESSING Press grated ginger between two spoons over screw-top jar; discard fibres. Add remaining ingredients; shake well.

serves 4
per serving 20.1g total fat (3.6g saturated fat); 1329kJ (318 cal); 5.2g carbohydrate; 29.1g protein; 3.5g fibre

beans and fennel salsa verde

¼ cup (60ml) olive oil

3 baby fennel bulbs (390g), trimmed, quartered

½ cup (125ml) chicken stock

300g baby green beans, trimmed

6 green onions, cut into 8cm lengths

1 teaspoon finely grated lemon rind

1 tablespoon lemon juice

6 anchovy fillets, drained, chopped finely

1 clove garlic, crushed

1 teaspoon dijon mustard

2 tablespoons finely chopped fresh flat-leaf parsley

1 Heat 2 teaspoons of the oil in medium frying pan; cook fennel, stirring, 2 minutes. Add stock, reduce heat; simmer, covered, about 5 minutes or until fennel is almost tender.

2 Add beans; simmer, covered, until beans are just tender. Add remaining oil and remaining ingredients; stir until heated through.

serves 4
per serving 12.2g total fat (1.8g saturated fat); 606kJ (145 cal); 4.8g carbohydrate; 4.1g protein; 4.2 fibre

PREPARATION TIME
10 MINS

tuna, bean and tomato salad

1 Place balsamic dressing ingredients in screw-top jar; shake well.
2 Place ingredients and dressing in large bowl; toss gently to combine.

serves 4
per serving 20.6g total fat (3.9g saturated fat); 1204kJ (288 cal);
10.6g carbohydrate; 15g protein; 6g fibre

185g can tuna in springwater, drained

300g can red kidney beans, drained, rinsed

1 small red onion (100g), sliced thinly

250g cherry tomatoes, halved

½ cup coarsely chopped fresh basil

1 medium avocado (250g), sliced thickly

100g baby rocket leaves

BALSAMIC DRESSING

2 tablespoons olive oil

1 tablespoon balsamic vinegar

1 teaspoon finely grated lemon rind

1 tablespoon lemon juice

1 teaspoon dijon mustard

1 clove garlic, crushed

ginger-glazed baby carrots

800g baby carrots

20g butter

1cm piece fresh ginger (5g), grated

¼ cup (60ml) fresh orange juice

2 teaspoons fresh chervil leaves

1 Boil, steam or microwave carrots until tender; drain.
2 Cook butter, ginger and juice in medium frying pan over medium heat, uncovered, 1 minute. Add carrots; toss gently to coat in butter mixture.
3 Serve carrots sprinkled with chervil.

serves 4
per serving 4.3g total fat (2.7g saturated fat); 347kJ (83 cal); 10g carbohydrate; 1.2g protein; 5.4g fibre

[
PREPARATION TIME
10 MINS
COOKING TIME
5 MINS
]

caprese salad

1 Arrange tomato and cheese alternately on serving platter.
2 Drizzle with oil; sprinkle with basil, and salt and pepper, if desired.

serves 4
per serving 20.6g total fat (8.8g saturated fat); 1007kJ (241 cal); 1.2g carbohydrate; 13.4g protein; 0.8g fibre

3 large egg tomatoes (270g), sliced thinly

5 bocconcini (300g), sliced thinly

2 tablespoons olive oil

⅓ cup loosely packed fresh basil leaves

PREPARATION TIME
15 MINS

PAN-FRIES + STIR-FRIES

> **PREPARATION TIME**
> **10 MINS**
> **COOKING TIME**
> **15 MINS**

black bean, beef and asparagus stir-fry

1 tablespoon rice vinegar

1 tablespoon soy sauce

1 tablespoon dry sherry

2 cloves garlic, crushed

750g beef strips

2 tablespoons peanut oil

2 tablespoons salted dried black beans

2 medium brown onions (300g), sliced thickly

500g asparagus, trimmed, halved

1 teaspoon cornflour

2 tablespoons oyster sauce

⅓ cup (80ml) beef stock

1 Combine vinegar, soy sauce, sherry and garlic in large bowl, add beef; toss beef to coat in mixture.
2 Heat half of the oil in wok; stir-fry beef, in batches, until browned.
3 Rinse beans; drain, mash with fork in small bowl. Heat remaining oil in same wok; stir-fry beans, onion and asparagus until onion just softens. Return beef to wok with blended cornflour, oyster sauce and stock; stir-fry until mixture boils and thickens slightly.

serves 4
per serving 16.4g total fat (4.7g saturated fat); 1501kJ (359 cal); 6.9g carbohydrate; 44.4g protein; 2.4g fibre

haloumi salad on turkish bread

1 Strain antipasto over small bowl; reserve ⅓-cup of the oil. Slice antipasto thickly. Drain artichokes; cut into quarters.
2 Cut cheese into eight slices. Heat 1 tablespoon of the reserved oil in medium frying pan; cook cheese until browned both sides.
3 Meanwhile, cut bread into 1cm slices; toast bread both sides.
4 Divide toasted bread among serving plates; top with rocket, antipasto, artichoke, tomatoes and cheese. Drizzle with combined vinegar and remaining reserved oil; sprinkle with nuts.

270g jar char-grilled antipasto

170g jar marinated artichoke hearts

250g haloumi cheese

½ loaf turkish bread (215g)

200g baby rocket leaves

250g yellow teardrop tomatoes

¼ cup (60ml) balsamic vinegar

2 tablespoons toasted pine nuts

serves 4
per serving 40.7g total fat (10g saturated fat); 2780kJ (665 cal); 34.8g carbohydrate; 24.5g protein; 10g fibre

fish with herb and tomato dressing

We used blue eye in this recipe, but you can use any firm white fish, such as perch or ling.

12 baby new potatoes (480g), halved

4 medium green zucchini (480g), quartered

2 tablespoons olive oil

4 white fish fillets (800g)

2 medium egg tomatoes (150g), chopped finely

2 tablespoons lemon juice

1 tablespoon finely chopped fresh dill

2 tablespoons finely chopped fresh basil

1 Boil, steam or microwave potato and zucchini, separately, until tender; drain.
2 Meanwhile, heat half of the oil in large non-stick frying pan; cook fish until cooked as desired. Remove from pan; cover to keep warm.
3 Heat remaining oil in same cleaned pan; cook tomato and juice, stirring, 2 minutes. Remove from heat; stir in herbs.
4 Divide fish and vegetables among serving plates; drizzle with tomato mixture.

serves 4
per serving 10.8g total fat (1.5g saturated fat); 1371kJ (328 cal); 18.5g carbohydrate; 38.1g protein; 4.6g fibre

pork butterfly steaks with radicchio

1 Sprinkle both sides of pork with seeds. Heat half of the oil in large frying pan; cook pork until cooked as desired. Remove from pan; cover to keep warm.
2 Meanwhile, cut radicchio in quarters; remove cores. Halve each quarter lengthways.
3 Cook bacon in same pan, stirring, until crisp. Add radicchio, remaining oil and remaining ingredients; cook, stirring, until radicchio just wilts.
4 Serve pork with hot radicchio mixture.

serves 4
per serving 27.7g total fat (7.5g saturated fat); 2006kJ (480 cal); 3.8g carbohydrate; 53.7g protein; 4.1g fibre

4 pork butterfly steaks (800g)

1 teaspoon fennel seeds, crushed

2 tablespoons olive oil

4 small radicchio (600g)

3 bacon rashers (210g), rind removed, chopped coarsely

2 cloves garlic, crushed

4 small egg tomatoes (240g), sliced thickly

1 tablespoon red wine vinegar

1 teaspoon brown sugar

pork and lemon grass stir-fry

1 tablespoon peanut oil

10cm stick (20g) finely chopped fresh lemon grass

2 fresh small red thai chillies, chopped finely

2 teaspoons finely grated fresh galangal

2 cloves garlic, crushed

500g pork mince

1 tablespoon thai red curry paste

100g green beans, trimmed, chopped coarsely

2 tablespoons fish sauce

2 tablespoons lime juice

1 tablespoon grated palm sugar

1 small red onion (100g), sliced thinly

2 green onions, sliced thinly

¼ cup loosely packed fresh thai basil leaves

¼ cup firmly packed fresh coriander leaves

¼ cup (35g) toasted peanuts, chopped coarsely

4 large iceberg lettuce leaves

1 Heat oil in wok; stir-fry lemon grass, chilli, galangal and garlic until fragrant. Add pork; stir-fry about 5 minutes or until pork changes colour. Add paste; cook, stirring, until fragrant.
2 Add beans, sauce, juice and sugar to wok; stir-fry about 5 minutes or until beans are just tender. Remove from heat; stir in onion, herbs and half of the nuts.
3 Divide lettuce leaves among serving plates; spoon pork mixture into lettuce leaves, sprinkle with remaining nuts.

serves 4
per serving 19.5g total fat (4.9g saturated fat); 1350kJ (323 cal); 7.2g carbohydrate; 29.8g protein; 3.7g fibre

prawn, asparagus and sesame stir-fry

1 Shell and devein prawns, leaving tails intact.
2 Heat half of the peanut oil in wok; stir-fry ginger, garlic and onion until fragrant. Add asparagus; stir-fry until tender. Remove from wok.
3 Heat remaining peanut oil in same wok; cook prawns, in batches, until cooked through. Return prawns to wok with asparagus mixture, chilli and combined wine, sauce, sesame oil and sugar; stir-fry until mixture is heated through. Serve stir-fry sprinkled with seeds.

serves 4
per serving 8.5g total fat (1.4g saturated fat); 907kJ (217 cal); 4.7g carbohydrate; 28.7g protein; 1.8g fibre

1kg uncooked large king prawns

1 tablespoon peanut oil

5cm piece fresh ginger (25g), grated

2 cloves garlic, crushed

1 medium brown onion (150g), sliced thinly

300g asparagus, trimmed, chopped coarsely

1 fresh long red chilli, sliced thinly

2 tablespoons rice wine

¼ cup (60ml) soy sauce

2 teaspoons sesame oil

2 teaspoons brown sugar

2 teaspoons toasted sesame seeds

fennel-seasoned steak with fried green tomatoes

2 teaspoons fennel seeds

1 teaspoon sea salt

½ teaspoon cracked black pepper

⅓ cup (80ml) olive oil

4 beef scotch fillet steaks (800g)

4 large green egg tomatoes (360g)

¼ cup (35g) plain flour

1 egg

2 tablespoons milk

½ cup (85g) polenta

2 tablespoons dijonnaise

50g wild rocket

1 Using mortar and pestle, coarsely crush seeds, salt and pepper; stir in half of the oil. Rub fennel mixture into beef.

2 Cut tomatoes into 1.5cm slices. Toss slices in flour; shake away excess flour. Dip slices into combined egg and milk; coat in polenta.

3 Heat remaining oil in large frying pan; cook slices until browned lightly both sides and just tender.

4 Cook beef on heated oiled grill plate (or grill or barbecue) until cooked as desired. Cover beef; stand 5 minutes.

5 Serve beef with tomato, dijonnaise and rocket.

serves 4
per serving 25.6g total fat (8.7g saturated fat); 2554kJ (611 cal); 25.2g carbohydrate; 48g protein; 2.2g fibre

chicken with pistachio sauce and kumara mash

1 Boil, steam or microwave kumara until tender; drain.
2 Meanwhile, slice chicken breasts in half horizontally. Heat oil and half of the butter in large frying pan; cook chicken, in batches, until cooked through. Cover to keep warm.
3 Place wine in same pan; bring to a boil. Stir in stock and cream, reduce heat; simmer, uncovered, about 10 minutes or until sauce thickens slightly. Stir in the hot water, thyme and nuts.
4 Meanwhile boil, steam or microwave beans until tender; drain.
5 Mash kumara with milk and remaining butter in medium bowl.
6 Serve chicken and sauce with kumara mash and beans.

serves 4
per serving 30.7g total fat (14.8g saturated fat); 2525kJ (604 cal); 30g carbohydrate; 47.3g protein; 6.2g fibre

2 medium kumara (800g), chopped coarsely

4 single chicken breast fillets (680g)

2 teaspoons olive oil

20g butter

½ cup (125ml) dry white wine

½ cup (125ml) chicken stock

⅔ cup (160ml) cream

2 tablespoons hot water

2 teaspoons fresh lemon thyme leaves

¼ cup (35g) toasted shelled pistachios, chopped coarsely

350g green beans

⅓ cup (80ml) hot milk

thai lime chicken with bok choy

1 tablespoon peanut oil

8 chicken thigh fillets (880g)

1 tablespoon fish sauce

2 tablespoons lime juice

2 tablespoons grated palm sugar

1 clove garlic, crushed

1 fresh small red thai chilli, chopped finely

300g baby bok choy, quartered lengthways

1 lime, cut into four slices

2 green onions, sliced thinly

¼ cup firmly packed fresh coriander leaves

1 Heat oil in large frying pan; cook chicken, in batches, until cooked through.
2 Meanwhile, place sauce, juice, sugar, garlic and chilli in screw-top jar; shake well.
3 Boil, steam or microwave bok choy until tender; drain.
4 Add lime slices to same large frying pan; cook until browned both sides.
5 Divide chicken among serving plates; spoon dressing over chicken, top with onion and coriander. Serve with bok choy, lime slices and steamed jasmine rice, if desired.

serves 4
per serving 20.7g total fat (5.7g saturated fat); 1622kJ (388 cal); 7.9g carbohydrate; 42.5g protein; 1.8g fibre

chicken and oyster sauce noodle stir-fry

1 Place noodles in large heatproof bowl, cover with boiling water, stand until just tender; drain. Cover to keep warm.

2 Meanwhile, heat half of the combined oils in wok; stir-fry chicken, in batches, until cooked through.

3 Heat remaining combined oils in same wok; stir-fry asparagus, corn and garlic until just tender. Return chicken to wok with noodles, sauce and chives; stir-fry until heated through.

serves 4
per serving 20.2g total fat (4.6g saturated fat); 2780kJ (665 cal); 80.1g carbohydrate; 39.6g protein; 6.9g fibre

375g dried rice stick noodles

2 teaspoons sesame oil

1 tablespoon peanut oil

600g chicken thigh fillets, sliced thinly

350g asparagus, trimmed, chopped coarsely

375g fresh baby corn, halved lengthways

2 cloves garlic, crushed

¼ cup (60ml) oyster sauce

½ cup coarsely chopped fresh garlic chives

hoisin beef stir-fry with cabbage

You need half a medium chinese cabbage weighing approximately 500g for this recipe.

¼ cup (60ml) peanut oil

4 cups (320g) coarsely shredded chinese cabbage

½ cup coarsely chopped fresh garlic chives

750g beef strips

1 large red onion (300g), sliced thickly

2 cloves garlic, crushed

1cm piece fresh ginger (5g), grated

1 teaspoon five-spice powder

250g fresh shiitake mushrooms, sliced thickly

1 large red capsicum (350g), sliced thinly

½ cup (125ml) hoisin sauce

1 tablespoon soy sauce

1 tablespoon rice wine vinegar

1 Heat 1 tablespoon of the oil in wok; stir-fry cabbage and chives until cabbage is wilted. Remove from wok; cover to keep warm.

2 Heat 1 tablespoon of the remaining oil in same wok; stir-fry beef, in batches, until browned.

3 Heat remaining oil in same wok; stir-fry onion until soft. Add garlic, ginger, five-spice, mushrooms and capsicum; stir-fry until vegetables are tender. Return beef to wok with sauces and vinegar; stir-fry until heated through. Serve cabbage mixture with stir-fry.

serves 4
per serving 22.9g total fat (5.8g saturated fat); 2082kJ (498 cal); 27.9g carbohydrate; 46g protein; 8.4g fibre

stir-fried beef and mixed mushrooms

1 Heat half of the peanut oil in wok; stir-fry beef, in batches, until browned.
2 Heat remaining peanut oil in same wok; stir-fry onion until soft. Add garlic, ginger, chilli and mushrooms; stir-fry until mushrooms are just tender.
3 Meanwhile, place noodles in large heatproof bowl, cover with boiling water, separate with fork; drain.
4 Return beef to wok with noodles and remaining ingredients; stir-fry until mixture boils and thickens slightly.

serves 4
per serving 29.9g total fat (8.9g saturated fat); 3298kJ (789 cal); 70.1g carbohydrate; 59.2g protein; 6.6g fibre

¼ cup (60ml) peanut oil

800g beef rump steak, sliced thinly

1 medium brown onion (150g), sliced thickly

2 cloves garlic, crushed

2cm piece fresh ginger (10g), grated

2 fresh long red chillies, sliced thinly

150g oyster mushrooms, halved

100g fresh shiitake mushrooms, halved

100g enoki mushrooms

450g hokkien noodles

6 green onions, sliced thickly

¼ cup (60ml) oyster sauce

1 tablespoon kecap manis

1 teaspoon sesame oil

GRILLS + BARBECUES

[PREPARATION TIME
20 MINS
COOKING TIME
15 MINS]

balsamic lamb with fattoush

8 lamb loin chops (800g)

¼ cup (60ml) balsamic vinegar

1 tablespoon olive oil

2 cloves garlic, crushed

FATTOUSH

2 large pitta

1 lebanese cucumber (130g), seeded, sliced thinly

3 medium tomatoes (450g), seeded, sliced thinly

1 small red onion (100g), sliced thinly

2 green onions, sliced thickly

2 tablespoons olive oil

¼ cup (60ml) lemon juice

1 clove garlic, crushed

½ teaspoon sweet paprika

1 Brush lamb with combined vinegar, oil and garlic. Cook lamb on heated oiled grill plate (or grill or barbecue) until cooked as desired. Cover to keep warm.

2 Meanwhile, make fattoush.

3 Serve lamb with fattoush.

FATTOUSH Preheat oven to hot. Toast bread in hot oven about 5 minutes or until crisp. Place remaining ingredients in large bowl. Break bread into pieces over salad; toss gently to combine.

serves 4
per serving 27.9g total fat (8.4g saturated fat); 2098kJ (502 cal); 24.6g carbohydrate; 37.3g protein; 3.5g fibre

steak and aïoli open sandwiches

8 beef fillet steaks (1kg)

4 large egg tomatoes (360g), halved lengthways

1 tablespoon olive oil

4 thick slices ciabatta (140g)

1 tablespoon finely shredded fresh basil

1 tablespoon balsamic vinegar

100g mesclun

AIOLI

1 clove garlic, crushed

½ cup (150g) whole-egg mayonnaise

1 Preheat grill.
2 Cook beef on heated oiled grill plate (or grill or barbecue) until cooked as desired. Cover, stand 5 minutes.
3 Meanwhile, place tomato, cut-side up, on oiled oven tray; drizzle with oil. Place under preheated grill about 10 minutes or until softened.
4 Meanwhile, combine aïoli ingredients in small bowl.
5 Toast bread both sides. Spread bread with aïoli; top with beef and tomato, sprinkle with basil and vinegar. Serve with mesclun.

serves 4
per serving 46.7g total fat (10.1g saturated fat); 3031kJ (725 cal); 18g carbohydrate; 58.7g protein; 2.6g fibre

PREPARATION TIME
15 MINS
COOKING TIME
15 MINS

pork and corn salsa tortilla wraps

1 Combine oil and seasoning in medium bowl, add pork; toss pork to coat in mixture. Cook pork in large heated non-stick frying pan until cooked as desired.
2 Meanwhile, warm tortillas according to manufacturer's instructions.
3 Combine corn, tomato, onion and coriander in medium bowl.
4 Divide pork, salsa and remaining ingredients among tortillas; roll to enclose filling.

serves 4
per serving 24.6g total fat (8.8g saturated fat); 2395kJ (573 cal); 46.1g carbohydrate; 41.5g protein; 8.4g fibre

2 tablespoons vegetable oil

35g packet taco seasoning mix

600g pork fillet, sliced thinly

16 corn tortillas

310g can corn kernels, drained

3 medium tomatoes (450g), chopped coarsely

1 small red onion (100g), chopped finely

½ cup coarsely chopped fresh coriander

1 butter lettuce, torn

½ cup (120g) light sour cream

chicken, lemon and artichoke skewers

You need to soak 12 bamboo skewers in water for a least 30 minutes before use to prevent splintering and scorching.

2 tablespoons lemon juice

2 tablespoons olive oil

2 cloves garlic, crushed

2 medium lemons (280g)

500g chicken breast fillets, diced into 3cm pieces

2 x 400g cans artichoke hearts, drained, halved

24 button mushrooms (300g)

1 Place juice, oil and garlic in screw-top jar; shake well.
2 Cut lemons into 24 pieces. Thread chicken, artichoke, mushrooms and lemon onto 12 skewers. Cook skewers on heated oiled grill plate (or grill or barbecue) until chicken is cooked through, brushing skewers with juice mixture while cooking.

serves 4
per serving 12.8g total fat (2g saturated fat); 1170kJ (280 cal); 4.5g carbohydrate; 34.2g protein; 7.7g fibre

salmon with garlic ginger butter

1 Cook salmon on heated oiled grill plate (or grill or barbecue) until cooked as desired.
2 Meanwhile, stir remaining ingredients in small saucepan over low heat until butter melts.
3 Spoon butter mixture over salmon and serve with steamed rice and baby bok choy, if desired.

serves 6
per serving 36.2g total fat (17g saturated fat); 2128kJ (509 cal); 3g carbohydrate; 43.6g protein; 0.3g fibre

6 salmon fillets (1.3kg)

150g butter, chopped

2 tablespoons soy sauce

2 cloves garlic, crushed

6cm piece fresh ginger (30g), grated

1 tablespoon brown sugar

1 teaspoon finely grated lemon rind

2 tablespoons lemon juice

barbecue chicken with nam jim

8 chicken thigh cutlets (1.3kg)

⅓ cup (90g) grated palm sugar

2 teaspoons ground cumin

1 cup loosely packed fresh mint leaves

1 cup loosely packed fresh thai basil leaves

NAM JIM

2 cloves garlic, quartered

3 long green chillies, chopped coarsely

2 coriander roots

2 tablespoons fish sauce

2 tablespoons grated palm sugar

3 shallots (75g), chopped coarsely

¼ cup (60ml) lime juice

1 Cut two deep slashes through skin and flesh of chicken; rub chicken with combined sugar and cumin.
2 Cook chicken on heated oiled grill plate (or grill or barbecue) until chicken is cooked through.
3 Meanwhile, blend or process nam jim ingredients until smooth.
4 Serve chicken with herbs and nam jim.

serves 4
per serving 32.9g total fat (10.7g saturated fat); 2387kJ (571 cal); 30.2g carbohydrate; 39.8g protein; 1.8g fibre

glazed pork cutlets with celeriac salad

1 Whisk honey, mustard and oil in large bowl, add pork; toss pork to coat in mixture. Cook pork on heated oiled grill plate (or grill or barbecue) until cooked as desired. Cover pork; stand 5 minutes.
2 Meanwhile, boil, steam or microwave carrots until just tender; drain. Cover to keep warm.
3 Combine celeriac, mayonnaise, garlic, sour cream, juice, parsley and extra mustard in medium bowl.
4 Serve cutlets with carrots and salad.

serves 4
per serving 37.8g total fat (9.6g saturated fat); 2441kJ (584 cal); 15.5g carbohydrate; 45.6g protein; 9g fibre

2 teaspoons honey

1 teaspoon dijon mustard

1 tablespoon olive oil

4 pork cutlets (1kg)

400g baby carrots, trimmed

650g celeriac, grated coarsely

⅓ cup (100g) whole egg mayonnaise

1 clove garlic, crushed

⅓ cup (80g) light sour cream

2 tablespoons lemon juice

½ cup coarsely chopped fresh flat-leaf parsley

2 teaspoons dijon mustard, extra

lamb patties with beetroot and tzatziki

500g lamb mince

1 small brown onion (80g), chopped finely

1 medium carrot (120g), grated coarsely

1 egg

2 tablespoons finely chopped fresh flat-leaf parsley

1 teaspoon finely grated lemon rind

½ teaspoon dried oregano leaves

2 cloves garlic, crushed

½ cup (140g) yogurt

1 lebanese cucumber (130g), seeded, chopped finely

1 tablespoon finely chopped fresh mint

1 loaf turkish bread (430g)

1 cup (60g) coarsely shredded cos lettuce

225g can sliced beetroot, drained

1 lemon (140g), cut into wedges

1 Using hand, combine lamb, onion, carrot, egg, parsley, rind, oregano and half of the garlic in medium bowl; shape lamb mixture into four patties. Cook patties on heated oiled grill plate (or grill or barbecue) until cooked as desired.

2 Meanwhile, combine yogurt, cucumber, mint and remaining garlic in small bowl. Cut bread into four pieces; split each piece in half horizontally. Toast bread cut-side up.

3 Sandwich lettuce, patties, yogurt mixture and beetroot between bread pieces. Serve with lemon wedges.

serves 4
per serving 19.3g total fat (6.9g saturated fat); 2441kJ (584 cal); 35.6g carbohydrate; 35.8g protein; 3.6g fibre

char-grilled veal and vegetables with tomato and caper salsa

1 Cook eggplant and zucchini, in batches, on heated oiled grill plate (or grill or barbecue) until browned and tender, brushing with 2 tablespoons of the oil. Cover to keep warm.
2 Sprinkle veal with pepper; cook on same heated grill plate until cooked as desired.
3 Meanwhile, combine tomato, onion, garlic, capers, vinegar and remaining oil in small bowl.
4 Serve eggplant, zucchini, veal and salsa sprinkled with basil.

TIP Antipasto eggplant and zucchini may be used instead of fresh for a quicker alternative.

serves 6
per serving 15.7g total fat (3.2g saturated fat); 1722kJ (412 cal); 4.5g carbohydrate; 62.3g protein; 3.4g fibre

6 baby eggplant (360g), halved lengthways

6 small zucchini (540g), halved lengthways

¼ cup (60ml) olive oil

12 veal cutlets (2kg)

1 tablespoon cracked black pepper

2 medium tomatoes (300g), seeded, chopped finely

1 small red onion (100g), chopped finely

1 clove garlic, crushed

2 tablespoons baby capers, drained, rinsed

1 tablespoon balsamic vinegar

1 tablespoon fresh baby basil leaves

fish with thai-style dressing

100g snow pea sprouts, trimmed

1 cup loosely packed fresh mint leaves

½ cup loosely packed fresh coriander leaves

3 shallots (75g), sliced thinly

2 fresh long red chillies, sliced thinly

4 firm white fish fillets (800g)

⅓ cup (80ml) lime juice

2 tablespoons grated palm sugar

1 tablespoon fish sauce

1 Combine sprouts, mint, coriander, shallots and chilli in medium bowl.
2 Cook fish on heated oiled grill plate (or grill or barbecue) until cooked as desired.
3 Meanwhile, combine juice, sugar and sauce in small bowl.
4 Serve fish with salad drizzled with dressing.

serves 4
per serving 1.6g total fat (0.3g saturated fat); 907kJ (217 cal); 13g carbohydrate; 36.8g protein; 2.6g fibre

PASTA

creamy pesto chicken with gnocchi

Fresh gnocchi is available in the refrigerated sections of most supermarkets.

900g chicken thigh fillets

1 tablespoon olive oil

2 cloves garlic, crushed

2 shallots (50g), chopped finely

100g fresh shiitake mushrooms, sliced thickly

½ cup (125ml) dry white wine

¼ cup (70g) sun-dried tomato pesto

300ml light cream

⅓ cup coarsely chopped fresh basil

625g fresh gnocchi

1 Cut each chicken fillet into thirds. Heat oil in large frying pan; cook chicken, in batches, until cooked through. Cover to keep warm.

2 Add garlic, shallot and mushroom to same pan; cook, stirring, 2 minutes. Stir in wine; simmer, uncovered, until liquid is almost evaporated. Stir in pesto and cream; bring mixture to a boil. Remove from heat; stir in basil.

3 Meanwhile, cook gnocchi, uncovered, in large saucepan of boiling water until gnocchi are just tender and float to the surface; drain.

4 Divide chicken and gnocchi among serving plates; drizzle with creamy pesto.

serves 4
per serving 49.2g total fat (20.9g saturated fat); 3678kJ (880 cal); 52.1g carbohydrate; 52.9g protein; 5g fibre

greek lamb and pasta salad

Originally a Neapolitan pasta, tortiglioni are a short pasta not unlike rigatoni or penne, having grooves on the outside surface and a wide internal cavity, both of which combine to make it a perfect pasta for holding sauces.

1 Combine lamb, oil and about a third of the oregano in large bowl. Cook lamb, in batches, in oiled non-stick frying pan until browned and cooked as desired. Cover lamb; stand 5 minutes, slice thinly.
2 Meanwhile, cook pasta in large saucepan of boiling water, uncovered, until just tender; drain. Rinse under cold water; drain.
3 Meanwhile, place lemon and oregano dressing ingredients in screw-top jar; shake well.
4 Place lamb and pasta in large bowl with onion, tomato, cucumber, capsicum, olives and dressing; toss gently to combine. Top with cheese; sprinkle with remaining oregano.

serves 6
per serving 40.1g total fat (12.4g saturated fat); 3357kJ (803 cal); 71.7g carbohydrate; 38.3g protein; 7.3g fibre

600g lamb fillets

1 tablespoon olive oil

1 tablespoon finely chopped fresh oregano

500g tortiglioni

1 medium red onion (170g), cut into thin wedges

500g cherry tomatoes, halved

2 lebanese cucumbers (260g), chopped coarsely

1 large green capsicum (350g), chopped coarsely

1⅔ cups (200g) seeded kalamata olives

200g fetta cheese, crumbled

LEMON AND OREGANO DRESSING

½ cup (125ml) olive oil

½ cup (125ml) lemon juice

1 tablespoon finely chopped fresh oregano

ricotta and spinach ravioli with pumpkin sauce

¼ cup (60ml) olive oil

1 small brown onion (80g), chopped finely

1 clove garlic, crushed

600g pumpkin, sliced thinly

1½ cups (375ml) chicken stock

½ teaspoon ground nutmeg

½ cup (125ml) cream

½ cup (125ml) hot water

600g fresh spinach and ricotta ravioli

⅓ cup (50g) toasted pine nuts

2 tablespoons coarsely chopped fresh chives

1 Heat half of the oil in large frying pan; cook onion and garlic, stirring, until onion softens. Remove from pan.
2 Heat remaining oil in same pan; cook pumpkin, in batches, until browned lightly. Return pumpkin and onion mixture to pan with stock and nutmeg; cook, stirring, until liquid is absorbed. Blend or process pumpkin mixture with cream and the hot water until smooth. Return to pan; stir, over low heat, until heated through.
3 Meanwhile, cook ravioli in large saucepan of boiling water, uncovered, until just tender; drain.
4 Serve pasta with pumpkin sauce, sprinkled with nuts and chives.

serves 4
per serving 42.3g total fat (13.6g saturated fat); 2391kJ (572 cal); 31.6g carbohydrate; 17.5g protein; 4.8g fibre

PREPARATION TIME
25 MINS
COOKING TIME
10 MINS

linguine with beans, potatoes and basil pesto

The generic name for Italian cheeses made from sheep milk is pecorino. It is a hard, white to pale yellow cheese having a slightly grainy texture and spicy, full flavour. Varieties are named after the region in which the cheese is produced: Romano from Rome, Sardo from Sardinia, Siciliano from Sicily, Toscano from Tuscany, etc. If unavailable, use parmesan.

1 Blend or process basil pesto ingredients until mixture forms a coarse paste.
2 Boil, steam or microwave beans and potato, separately, until just tender; drain.
3 Meanwhile, cook pasta in large saucepan of boiling water, uncovered, until just tender; drain, reserving ½-cup cooking liquid.
4 Combine beans, potato and pasta in large bowl. Stir reserved liquid into pesto; pour over pasta. Add cheese; toss gently to combine.

serves 4
per serving 45.3g total fat (9.9g saturated fat); 3867kJ (925 cal); 101.4g carbohydrate; 27.3g protein; 10.3g fibre

250g green beans, cut into 5cm lengths

2 medium potatoes (400g), sliced thinly lengthways

500g linguine

100g piece pecorino cheese, shaved

BASIL PESTO

1 cup firmly packed fresh basil leaves

¼ cup (20g) finely grated pecorino cheese

¼ cup (40g) toasted pine nuts

2 cloves garlic, crushed

½ cup (125ml) olive oil

chilli squid fettuccine

500g fresh fettuccine

½ cup (125ml) olive oil

450g small squid hoods, sliced thinly

2 fresh long red chillies, sliced thinly

2 cloves garlic, crushed

250g rocket leaves, torn

100g fetta cheese, crumbled

1 Cook pasta in large saucepan of boiling water, uncovered, until just tender.
2 Meanwhile, heat 1 tablespoon of the oil in large shallow frying pan; cook squid, in batches, over high heat, until tender and browned lightly.
3 Add remaining oil to pan with chilli and garlic; cook, stirring, until fragrant. Add rocket; cook, stirring, until just wilted.
4 Place drained pasta in large bowl with squid, rocket mixture and cheese; toss gently to combine.

serves 6
per serving 25g total fat (5.7g saturated fat); 2378kJ (569 cal); 59.7g carbohydrate; 26g protein; 5g fibre

PREPARATION TIME
15 MINS
COOKING TIME
25 MINS

asparagus, bacon and cheese pasta

1 Cook pasta in large saucepan of boiling water, uncovered, until just tender.
2 Meanwhile, boil, steam or microwave asparagus until just tender; drain.
3 Cook bacon in large heated non-stick frying pan, stirring, until crisp. Add garlic; cook, stirring, until fragrant.
4 Place drained pasta, asparagus and bacon mixture in large bowl with butter, cheeses and cream; toss gently to combine. Serve pasta sprinkled with parsley.

serves 4
per serving 31.2g total fat (17.9g saturated fat); 3240kJ (775 cal); 90g carbohydrate; 32.7g protein; 7.8g fibre

500g tortiglioni

500g asparagus, trimmed, chopped coarsely

5 bacon rashers (350g), rind removed, sliced thinly

1 clove garlic, crushed

50g butter, chopped

½ cup (40g) finely grated parmesan cheese

½ cup (50g) finely grated mozzarella cheese

⅓ cup (80ml) cream

¼ cup coarsely chopped fresh flat-leaf parsley

pappardelle chicken and creamy mushroom sauce

You need to buy a barbecued chicken weighing approximately 900g for this recipe. Discard skin and bones before shredding the chicken meat.

2 tablespoons olive oil

1 clove garlic, crushed

1 small brown onion (80g), chopped finely

250g swiss brown mushrooms, sliced thinly

¾ cup (180ml) cream

2 teaspoons finely chopped fresh rosemary

20g butter

500g pappardelle

3 cups (480g) coarsely shredded cooked chicken

½ cup (60g) coarsely chopped toasted walnuts

¼ cup coarsely chopped fresh flat-leaf parsley

¾ cup (60g) finely grated parmesan cheese

1 Heat oil in large frying pan; cook garlic and onion, stirring, until onion softens. Add mushroom; cook, stirring, until just tender.
2 Add cream and rosemary to pan; bring to a boil. Reduce heat; simmer, uncovered, until sauce thickens slightly. Add butter; stir until butter melts.
3 Meanwhile, cook pasta in large saucepan of boiling water, uncovered, until just tender; drain. Return to pan.
4 Add hot cream sauce, chicken, nuts, parsley and half of the cheese to hot pasta; toss gently to combine. Serve immediately, sprinkled with remaining cheese.

serves 4
per serving 55.7g total fat (21.5g saturated fat); 4548kJ (1088 cal); 91.5g carbohydrate; 54.9g protein; 9.3g fibre

bavette with prawns, peas, lemon and dill

1 Shell and devein prawns; halve lengthways.
2 Cook pasta in large saucepan of boiling water, uncovered, until just tender; drain. Return to pan.
3 Meanwhile, heat half of the oil in large frying pan; cook garlic and prawns, in batches, until prawns are just changed in colour. Cover to keep warm.
4 Place peas in same frying pan; cook, stirring, until heated through. Add rind, onion and dill; cook, stirring, until onion is just tender. Return prawns to frying pan with juice; stir until heated through. Add prawn mixture and remaining oil to hot pasta; toss gently to combine.

serves 4
per serving 15.7g total fat (2.3g saturated fat); 2441kJ (584 cal); 69.8g carbohydrate; 39.2g protein; 8g fibre

1kg uncooked large king prawns

375g bavette

2 tablespoons olive oil

2 cloves garlic, crushed

1½ cups (180g) frozen peas

2 teaspoons finely grated lemon rind

6 green onions, sliced thinly

1 tablespoon coarsely chopped fresh dill

¼ cup (60ml) lemon juice

rigatoni bolognese

1 medium brown onion (150g), chopped coarsely

1 small carrot (70g) chopped coarsely

1 trimmed celery stalk (100g), chopped coarsely

1 tablespoon olive oil

50g butter

2 cloves garlic, crushed

2 Italian-style sausages (170g)

500g veal and pork mince

2 tablespoons tomato paste

½ cup (125ml) dry white wine

¼ cup (60ml) beef stock

425g can crushed tomatoes

2 tablespoons finely chopped fresh basil

2 tablespoons finely chopped fresh flat-leaf parsley

500g rigatoni

¼ cup (20g) coarsely grated parmesan cheese

1 Blend or process onion, carrot and celery until chopped finely.
2 Heat oil and butter in large saucepan, cook onion mixture and garlic, stirring occasionally, 5 minutes.
3 Meanwhile, squeeze filling from sausages; discard casings. Add sausage filling and mince to pan; cook, stirring, until meats are browned lightly.
4 Stir in paste and wine; bring to a boil. Reduce heat; simmer, uncovered, 2 minutes. Add stock and undrained tomatoes; return to a boil. Reduce heat; simmer, uncovered, about 20 minutes or until bolognese thickens. Stir in herbs.
5 Meanwhile, cook pasta in large saucepan of boiling water, uncovered, until just tender; drain.
6 Serve pasta topped with bolognese and sprinkle with cheese.

serves 4
per serving 36.9g total fat (16.5g saturated fat); 3933kJ (941 cal); 96.5g carbohydrate; 49.4g protein; 10.4g fibre

DESSERTS

strawberry meringue cream

500g strawberries, halved

1 tablespoon orange-flavoured liqueur

300ml thickened cream

2 tablespoons icing sugar mixture

½ cup (140g) yogurt

10 mini pavlova shells (100g), chopped coarsely

1 Combine strawberries and liqueur in medium bowl.
2 Beat cream and sugar in small bowl with electric mixer until soft peaks form. Fold in yogurt.
3 Place half of the strawberries in 1.25-litre (5-cup) serving dish. Top with half of the pavlova and half of the cream mixture. Repeat layering with remaining strawberries, pavlova and cream mixture.

serves 6
per serving 19.5g total fat (12.8g saturated fat); 1237kJ (296 cal); 25.2g carbohydrate; 4g protein; 1.8g fibre

caramelised apple tarts

1 sheet ready-rolled puff pastry, thawed

1 egg yolk

1 tablespoon milk

1 tablespoon caster sugar

2 large apples (400g)

60g butter, softened

⅓ cup (75g) firmly packed brown sugar

½ teaspoon ground cinnamon

1 Preheat oven to hot. Lightly grease oven tray.
2 Score pastry in crosshatch pattern with sharp knife. Brush pastry with combined yolk and milk; sprinkle with caster sugar. Cut into four squares; place on prepared tray.
3 Cut unpeeled apples crossways in 5mm slices. Place sliced apples, overlapping if necessary, over base of large baking dish; dot with butter, sprinkle with brown sugar and cinnamon. Bake pastry and apple slices, uncovered, in hot oven about 10 minutes or until pastry is puffed and browned. Remove pastry from oven. Turn apple slices; bake, uncovered, in hot oven about 10 minutes or until soft and browned.
4 Top pastry with apple; drizzle with caramel mixture in baking dish. Serve with frozen vanilla yogurt or ice-cream, if desired.

serves 4
per serving 23.5g total fat (13.8g saturated fat); 1751kJ (419 cal); 50.3g carbohydrate; 3.7g protein; 2.6g fibre

[PREPARATION TIME
15 MINS
COOKING TIME
20 MINS]

warm lemon meringue pots

1 Preheat oven to moderately hot.

2 Blend cornflour and sugar with juice and the water in small saucepan; stir over heat until mixture boils and thickens. Reduce heat; simmer, uncovered, 1 minute. Remove from heat; stir in rind, egg yolks, butter and cream.

3 Divide lemon mixture among four ½-cup (125ml) ovenproof dishes; place dishes on oven tray.

4 Meanwhile, beat egg whites in small bowl with electric mixer until soft peaks form; gradually add extra sugar, 1 tablespoon at a time, beating until sugar dissolves between additions. Spoon meringue evenly over lemon mixture.

5 Bake, uncovered, in moderately hot oven about 5 minutes or until meringue is browned lightly.

TIP This dessert is best served hot.

serves 4
per serving 12.5g total fat (7.3g saturated fat); 1363kJ (326 cal); 51.7g carbohydrate; 3.7g protein; 0.1g fibre

2 tablespoons cornflour

½ cup (110g) caster sugar

¼ cup (60ml) lemon juice

½ cup (125ml) water

1 teaspoon finely grated lemon rind

2 eggs, separated

30g butter, chopped

2 tablespoons cream

⅓ cup (75g) caster sugar, extra

PREPARATION TIME
10 MINS
COOKING TIME
15 MINS

sour cherry baked custards

Sour or morello cherries are available in jars. You can use any canned fruit of your choice.

1 cup (200g) drained morello cherries

3 eggs

1 teaspoon vanilla extract

½ cup (110g) caster sugar

2 cups (500ml) hot milk

2 teaspoons custard powder

1 tablespoon cold milk

½ teaspoon ground cinnamon

1 Preheat oven to moderately slow.
2 Pat dry cherries with absorbent paper; divide among four shallow ¾-cup (180ml) ovenproof dishes.
3 Whisk eggs, extract and sugar in medium bowl. Gradually whisk hot milk into egg mixture.
4 Blend custard powder with cold milk in small bowl until smooth; whisk into egg mixture.
5 Pour mixture over cherries; bake, uncovered, in moderately slow oven about 25 minutes or until just set. Serve warm or cooled sprinkled with cinnamon.

serves 4
per serving 9.1g total fat (4.6g saturated fat); 1137kJ (272 cal); 39.4g carbohydrate; 9.8g protein; 0.7g fibre

PREPARATION TIME
10 MINS
COOKING TIME
15 MINS

panettone with ricotta and caramelised peaches

Amaretto, originally from Italy, is an almond-flavoured liqueur and can be purchased from liquor stores.

1 Cut each peach into eight wedges. Cook peach and sugar in large non-stick frying pan about 5 minutes or until sugar dissolves. Reduce heat; simmer, uncovered, about 10 minutes or until peach is soft and pan juices are syrupy. Gently stir in liqueur.
2 Meanwhile, slice each panettone crossways into six pieces; toast panettone lightly both sides.
3 Divide panettone among serving plates; top with cheese and peach, drizzle with pan juices.

TIP If small panettone are unavailable, cut 7cm rounds from large panettone, brioche or fruit bread.

3 medium peaches (450g)

⅓ cup (75g) firmly packed brown sugar

2 teaspoons amaretto

2 x 100g panettone

1 cup (200g) ricotta cheese

serves 6
per serving 8.1g total fat (4.7g saturated fat); 949kJ (227 cal); 32.2g carbohydrate; 6.7g protein; 2g fibre

banana tarte tatin

50g butter

⅓ cup (75g) firmly packed
brown sugar

¼ cup (60ml) thickened cream

¼ teaspoon ground cinnamon

3 small bananas (390g),
sliced thinly

1 sheet ready-rolled puff
pastry, thawed

1 egg, beaten lightly

1 Preheat oven to hot.
2 Stir butter, sugar, cream and cinnamon in small saucepan, over low
  heat, until sugar dissolves; bring to a boil. Reduce heat; simmer,
  uncovered, 2 minutes.
3 Pour caramel sauce into 23cm pie dish; top with banana.
4 Trim corners from pastry sheet to form about 24cm circle. Place
  pastry sheet over banana, ease pastry into side of dish. Brush pastry
  with egg; bake, uncovered, in hot oven about 15 minutes or until
  pastry is browned.
5 Carefully turn tart onto serving plate; serve immediately.

TIP Serve with cream or ice-cream.

serves 6
per serving 17.8g total fat (10.6g saturated fat); 1241kJ (297 cal);
31.8g carbohydrate; 3.7g protein; 1.5g fibre

mocha creams

50g dark eating chocolate, chopped coarsely

300ml thickened cream

3 teaspoons instant coffee powder

1 tablespoon warm water

1 egg white

¼ cup (55g) caster sugar

⅓ cup (65g) scorched almonds, chopped coarsely

1 Stir chocolate and ¼ cup of the cream in small saucepan, over low heat, until smooth. Divide mixture among four ¾-cup (180ml) serving glasses; swirl chocolate to coat inside of the glasses. Refrigerate until required.

2 Stir coffee and the warm water in small bowl until coffee dissolves; cool 10 minutes. Beat remaining cream in small bowl with electric mixer until soft peaks form; fold in coffee mixture.

3 Beat egg white in small bowl with electric mixer until soft peaks form. Gradually add sugar, 1 tablespoon at time, beating until sugar dissolves between additions. Fold egg white mixture and ¼ cup of the nuts into cream mixture. Divide mixture among glasses; top with remaining nuts.

serves 4
per serving 36.5g total fat (22.6g saturated fat); 1960kJ (469 cal); 32.5g carbohydrate; 5.2g protein; 1g fibre

PREPARATION TIME
10 MINS
COOKING TIME
2 MINS

honeyed figs with toasted fruit bread

1 Spread both sides of bread with butter. Heat large frying pan; toast bread, uncovered, about 5 minutes or until browned both sides. Remove from pan.
2 Place sugar in small shallow bowl; press cut side of fig half in sugar. Place figs, sugar-side down, in same pan; cook, uncovered, about 5 minutes or until browned. Remove from pan.
3 Place any remaining sugar in same pan with the water; stir until hot. Serve bread with figs, pan juices and thick yogurt, if desired.

8 slices fruit bread (250g)

50g butter, softened

¼ cup (55g) firmly packed brown sugar

6 medium fresh figs (360g), halved

½ cup (125ml) water

serves 4
per serving 12.8g total fat (7.2g saturated fat); 1459kJ (349 cal); 53.7g carbohydrate; 6.1g protein; 4.9g fibre

PREPARATION TIME
5 MINS
COOKING TIME
10 MINS

mixed berries
with sponge fingers

12 savoiardi sponge finger
biscuits (140g)

1 cup (250ml) cranberry juice

400g french vanilla low-fat frûche

150g fresh raspberries

150g fresh blueberries

1 Dip biscuits in juice; divide among four 1½-cup (375ml) serving glasses. Sprinkle remaining juice over biscuits.

2 Divide half of the frûche mixture among glasses; sprinkle with half of the berries. Repeat layering with remaining frûche and remaining berries.

TIP This dessert can be prepared several hours in advance; store, covered, in refrigerator.

serves 4
per serving 2.1g total fat (0.7g saturated fat); 1095kJ (262 cal); 47g carbohydrate; 11.9g protein; 3.1g fibre

PREPARATION TIME

15 MINS

COOKING TIME

25 MINS

pecan and chocolate brownies

1. Preheat oven to moderately hot; grease eight holes of 12-hole (⅓-cup/80ml) muffin pan, line bases with rounds of baking paper.
2. Combine butter, chocolate and sugar in medium heavy-based saucepan; stir over low heat until smooth.
3. Transfer to large bowl; stir in egg, extract, sifted flour and cocoa then extra chocolate. Divide mixture among prepared holes; sprinkle with nuts. Bake, uncovered, in moderately hot oven about 20 minutes.

makes 8
per brownie 19.6g total fat (10.3g saturated fat); 1538kJ (368 cal); 45.1g carbohydrate; 4.9g protein; 1.1g fibre

80g butter, chopped

150g dark eating chocolate, chopped coarsely

¾ cup (165g) firmly packed brown sugar

2 eggs, beaten lightly

½ teaspoon vanilla extract

⅔ cup (100g) plain flour

1 tablespoon cocoa powder

50g dark eating chocolate, chopped coarsely, extra

¼ cup (30g) coarsely chopped pecans

lemon meringue sundae

²/₃ cup (220g) lemon butter

¹/₃ cup (80ml) cream

1 litre vanilla ice-cream

4 mini pavlova shells (40g), chopped coarsely

1 Stir lemon butter and cream in small saucepan, over low heat, until smooth; cool 10 minutes.
2 Layer ice-cream, lemon butter mixture and pavlova in four serving glasses.

TIP If you cannot find mini pavlova shells you could use part of whole meringue shell or coconut macaroons.

serve 4
per serving 23.5g total fat (14.5g saturated fat); 2048kJ (490 cal); 67.3g carbohydrate; 5.4g protein; 0.1g fibre

summer berry sundae

¼ cup (55g) caster sugar

500g mixed frozen berries

1 tablespoon orange-flavoured liqueur

1 litre vanilla ice-cream

²/₃ cup (100g) toasted macadamias, chopped coarsely

1 Stir sugar and berries in medium saucepan over heat, without boiling, until sugar dissolves; bring to a boil. Reduce heat; simmer, uncovered, about 5 minutes or until berries soften. Stir in liqueur; cool 10 minutes.
2 Layer ice-cream, berry mixture and nuts in four serving glasses.

TIP You can use orange juice instead of the liqueur for a non-alcoholic dessert.

serves 4
per serving 32.9g total fat (11.3g saturated fat); 2257kJ (540 cal); 52.9g carbohydrate; 7.3g protein; 6g fibre

mocha liqueur sundae

100g dark eating chocolate

⅔ cup (160ml) thickened cream

1 tablespoon coffee-flavoured liqueur

1 litre chocolate ice-cream

150g chocolate-coated coffee beans

1 Stir chocolate and cream in medium saucepan, over low heat, until mixture is smooth; stir in liqueur. Cool 10 minutes.
2 Layer ice-cream chocolate sauce and coffee beans in four serving glasses.

serve 4
per serving 45.9g total fat (28.9g saturated fat); 2905kJ (695 cal); 64.6g carbohydrate; 7.8g protein; 2.8g fibre

layered banana split with caramel sauce

⅔ cup (160ml) thickened cream

60g butter

¾ cup (165g) firmly packed brown sugar

1 cup (250ml) thickened cream, extra

2 large bananas (460g), sliced thinly

500ml vanilla ice-cream

½ cup (40g) toasted almond flakes

1 Stir cream, butter and sugar in small saucepan, over medium heat, until smooth. Reduce heat; simmer, uncovered, 2 minutes. Cool 10 minutes.
2 Meanwhile, beat extra cream in small bowl with electric mixer until soft peaks form.
3 Divide half of the sauce among four serving dishes; top with banana, cream and ice-cream then remaining sauce and nuts.

serves 4
per serving 62.2g total fat (37.8g saturated fat); 3595kJ (860 cal); 72.3g carbohydrate; 7.8g protein; 2.8g fibre

glossary

BABA GHANOUSH a Middle-Eastern salad or dip made from softened roasted eggplant, tahini, lemon juice, garlic and oil; available ready-made from most supermarkets.

BACON RASHERS also known as bacon slices.

BAMBOO SHOOTS the tender shoots of bamboo plants; available in cans, must be drained and rinsed before use.

BEAN SPROUTS also known as bean shoots; tender new growths of assorted beans and seeds grown for consumption as sprouts.

BEANS
green sometimes called french or string beans, this long fresh bean is consumed pod and all.
kidney medium-size red bean, slightly floury yet sweet in flavour; sold dried or canned.
salted black also known as chinese black beans; these are fermented and salted soy beans, available in cans and jars. Mash during cooking to release the flavour.
white many varieties of cooked white beans are available canned, among them are cannellini, butter and haricot beans; any of these can be used interchangeably.

BOK CHOY also known as bak choy, pak choi, chinese white cabbage or chinese chard, has a fresh, mild mustard taste; use stems and leaves, stir-fry or braised. Baby bok choy, also known as pak kat farang or shanghai bok choy, is small and more tender than bok choy.

CAPSICUM also known as bell pepper or, simply, pepper; can be red, green, yellow, orange or purplish black. Seeds and membranes should be discarded before use.

CAYENNE PEPPER a long, thin-fleshed, extremely hot dried red chilli, usually purchased ground.

CELERIAC tuberous root with brown skin, white flesh and a celery-like flavour. Also known as knob celery.

CHEESE
goat made from goat milk; has an earthy, strong taste. Available in both soft and firm textures; is sometimes rolled in ash or herbs.
haloumi a firm, cream-coloured sheep-milk cheese matured in brine; somewhat like a minty, salty fetta in flavour, haloumi can be grilled or fried, briefly, without breaking down.
pecorino is the generic Italian name for cheeses made from sheep milk. It's a hard, white to pale yellow cheese, usually matured for eight to 12 months, and known for the region in which it's produced - Romano from Rome, Sardo from Sardinia, Siciliano from Sicily and Toscano from Tuscany.

CHILLI available in many different types and sizes. Use rubber gloves when seeding and chopping fresh chillies as they can burn your skin. Removing seeds and membranes lessens the heat level.
green generally unripened thai chillies, but different varieties that are ripe when green may be used.
thai, red small, bright red, medium-hot chilli.

CHINESE CABBAGE also known as peking or napa cabbage, wong bok or petsai. Elongated in shape with pale green, crinkly leaves.

CHORIZO a sausage of Spanish origin, made of coarsely ground pork and highly seasoned with garlic and chillies.

CIABATTA in Italian, the word means slipper, which is the traditional shape of this popular white, crisp-crusted bread.

CORNFLOUR also known as cornstarch; used as a thickening agent in all types of cooking.

COUSCOUS a fine, grain-like cereal product made from semolina. Originally from North Africa.

CUCUMBER, LEBANESE short, slender and thin-skinned; this variety is also known as the burpless or European cucumber.

CUMIN also known as zeera, comes in seed or ground form; available from supermarkets.

CUSTARD POWDER instant mixture used to make pouring custard; similar to North American instant pudding mixes.

DIJONNAISE a bottled mixture of dijon mustard and mayonnaise; found in supermarkets.

EGGPLANT also known as aubergine; belongs to the same family as tomatoes, chillies and potatoes. Ranging in size from tiny to very large and in colour from pale green to deep purple, eggplant has an equally wide variety of flavours.

EGGS some recipes in this book call for raw or barely cooked eggs; exercise caution if there is a salmonella problem in your area.

FIVE-SPICE POWDER a fragrant mixture of star anise, ground cinnamon, cloves, sichuan pepper and fennel seeds.

FLOUR, PLAIN all-purpose flour, made from wheat.

FRUCHE a commercial dessert having less than 0.5g fat per 100g; fromage frais or a low-fat yogurt can be substituted if frûche is not available.

GALANGAL also known as ka, a rhizome with a hot ginger-citrusy flavour; used similarly to ginger and garlic as a seasoning and as an ingredient. Fresh ginger can be substituted for fresh galangal, but the flavour of the dish will not be the same.

GINGER also known as green or root ginger; the thick gnarled root of a tropical plant. Can be kept, peeled, covered with dry sherry, in a jar and refrigerated, or frozen in an airtight container.

HERBS when specified, we used dried (not ground) herbs in the proportion of 1:4 for fresh herbs (1 teaspoon dried herbs equals 4 teaspoons chopped fresh herbs).
chervil also known as cicily; mildly fennel-flavoured herb with curly dark-green leaves.
coriander also known as pak chee, cilantro or chinese parsley; bright-green-leafed herb with a pungent flavour. Both the stems and roots of coriander are used; wash well before chopping.
thai basil has smaller leaves and purplish stems, it has a slight licorice or aniseed taste, and is one of the basic flavours that typify Thai cuisine.
thyme a basic herb of French cuisine. Has tiny grey-green leaves that give off a pungent minty, light-lemon aroma.

KAFFIR LIME LEAVES look like two glossy dark green leaves joined end to end, forming an hourglass shape. Sold fresh, dried or frozen; dried leaves are less potent so double the number called for in a recipe if you substitute them for fresh leaves. A strip of fresh lime peel can be substituted for each kaffir lime leaf.

KUMARA Polynesian name of orange-fleshed sweet potato often confused with yam.

LEMON BUTTER lemon curd, lemon cheese or lemon spread.

LEMON GRASS a tall, clumping, lemon-smelling and tasting, sharp-edged grass; the white lower part of the stem is used, finely chopped, in cooking.

LETTUCE
mignonette has crisp, tightly furled leaves and a slightly bitter taste.
oak leaf also known as Feville de Chene. Available in both red and green leaf.

MESCLUN a salad mix of assorted young lettuce and other green leaves.

MUSHROOMS
shiitake when fresh are also known as chinese black, forest or golden oak mushrooms. Are large and meaty with the earthiness and taste of wild mushrooms. When dried, they are known as donko or dried chinese mushrooms; rehydrate before use.
swiss brown also known as roman or cremini; light-to dark-brown mushrooms with full-bodied flavour. Button or cap mushrooms can be substituted.

NUTMEG the dried nut of an evergreen tree native to Indonesia; it is available in ground form or you can grate your own with a fine grater.

PASTA
bavette a long, flat, narrow ribbon pasta that is similar to tagliatelle, only narrower.
pappardelle in Bologna, this is also called larghissime, which means "very wide". It is the widest ribbon pasta, and can be cut either straight or saw-edged.

rigatoni large, wide chewy macaroni, usually ridged on the surface.
tortiglioni a short pasta not unlike rigatoni or penne, having grooves on the outside surface and a wide internal cavity; a perfect pasta for holding creamy sauces.

PITTA also known as Lebanese bread. Is also available in small thick pieces called pocket pitta.

POLENTA also known as cornmeal; a flour-like cereal made of dried corn (maize) sold ground in several different textures. Also the name of the dish made from it.

PROSCIUTTO cured, air-dried (unsmoked), pressed ham; usually sold thinly sliced. Available from most delicatessens.

RADICCHIO a member of the chicory family. Has dark burgundy leaves and a strong bitter flavour.

SAFFRON available in strands or ground form; imparts a yellow-orange colour to food once infused. Quality varies greatly; the best is the most expensive spice in the world. Should be stored in the freezer.

SAUCES
fish also called nam pla or nuoc nam; made from pulverised salted fermented fish, most often anchovies. Has a pungent smell and strong taste, so use sparingly.
hoisin a thick, sweet and spicy Chinese paste made from fermented salted soy beans, onions and garlic; used as a marinade or baste.
kecap manis a dark, thick sweet soy sauce.

SAVOIARDI also known as ladyfingers, savoy biscuits or sponge finger biscuits; Italian-style crisp fingers made from sponge-cake mixture.

SHALLOTS also called french shallots, golden shallots or eschalots; small, elongated, brown-skinned members of the onion family.

SHERRY fortified wine consumed as an aperitif or used in cooking. Sold as fino (light, dry), amontillado (medium sweet, dark) and oloroso (full-bodied, very dark).

STOCK stock cubes, powder or concentrated liquid can be used. As a guide, 1 teaspoon of stock powder or 1 small crumbled stock cube or 1 portion stock concentrate mixed with 1 cup (250ml) water will give a fairly strong stock.

SUGAR we used coarse, granulated table sugar, also known as crystal sugar, unless otherwise specified.
brown an extremely soft, fine granulated sugar retaining molasses for its characteristic colour and flavour.
caster also known as superfine or finely granulated table sugar.
palm also known as nam tan pip, jaggery, jawa or gula melaka; made from the sap of the sugar palm tree. Light brown to black in colour and usually sold in rock-hard cakes; can be substituted with brown sugar, if unavailable.

TACO SEASONING MIX a packaged seasoning meant to duplicate the Mexican sauce made from oregano, cumin, chillies and other spices.

TORTILLA thin, round unleavened bread that originated in Mexico; two kinds are available, one made from wheat flour and the other from corn.

TURKISH BREAD also known as pide, comes in long (about 45cm) flat loaves as well as individual rounds.

VANILLA EXTRACT obtained from vanilla beans infused in water. A non-alcoholic version of essence.

VINEGAR
balsamic authentic only from the province of Modena, Italy; made from a regional wine of white trebbiano grapes specially processed then aged in antique wooden casks to give its exquisite flavour.
red wine based on fermented red wine.
rice a colourless vinegar made from fermented rice and flavoured with sugar and salt.
rice wine made from rice wine lees (sediment), salt and alcohol.
white made from spirit of cane sugar.
white wine made from white wine.

WATER CHESTNUTS resemble chestnut in appearance, hence the English name. Are small brown tubers with a crisp, white, nutty-tasting flesh. They are at their best fresh, however, canned water chestnuts are more easily obtained and can be kept about a month, once opened, under refrigeration.

WHOLE EGG MAYONNAISE a commercial mayonnaise of high quality made with whole eggs and labelled as such. Must be refrigerated after opening.

WONTON WRAPPERS also known as wonton skins; made of flour, eggs and water, they come in varying thicknesses. Found in the refrigerated section of Asian grocery stores or supermarkets. Gow gee, egg or spring roll pastry sheets can be substituted.

ZUCCHINI also known as courgette; small green, yellow or white vegetable belonging to the squash family.

index

facts + figures

Wherever you live, you'll be able to use our recipes with the help of these easy-to-follow conversions. While these conversions are approximate only, the difference between an exact and the approximate conversion of various liquid and dry measures is minimal and will not affect your cooking results.

LIQUID MEASURES

METRIC	IMPERIAL
30ml	1 fluid oz
60ml	2 fluid oz
100ml	3 fluid oz
125ml	4 fluid oz
150ml	5 fluid oz (¼ pint/1 gill)
190ml	6 fluid oz
250ml	8 fluid oz
300ml	10 fluid oz (½ pint)
500ml	16 fluid oz
600ml	20 fluid oz (1 pint)
1000ml (1 litre)	1¾ pints

MEASURING EQUIPMENT

The difference between one country's measuring cups and another's is, at most, within a 2 or 3 teaspoon variance. (For the record, one Australian metric measuring cup holds approximately 250ml.) The most accurate way of measuring dry ingredients is to weigh them. When measuring liquids, use a clear glass or plastic jug with the metric markings. (One Australian metric tablespoon holds 20ml; one Australian metric teaspoon holds 5ml.)

DRY MEASURES

METRIC	IMPERIAL
15g	½oz
30g	1oz
60g	2oz
90g	3oz
125g	4oz (¼lb)
155g	5oz
185g	6oz
220g	7oz
250g	8oz (½lb)
280g	9oz
315g	10oz
345g	11oz
375g	12oz (¾lb)
410g	13oz
440g	14oz
470g	15oz
500g	16oz (1lb)
750g	24oz (1½lb)
1kg	32oz (2lb)

HELPFUL MEASURES

METRIC	IMPERIAL
3mm	⅛in
6mm	¼in
1cm	½in
2cm	¾in
2.5cm	1in
5cm	2in
6cm	2½in
8cm	3in
10cm	4in
13cm	5in
15cm	6in
18cm	7in
20cm	8in
23cm	9in
25cm	10in
28cm	11in
30cm	12in (1ft)

HOW TO MEASURE

When using graduated metric measuring cups, shake dry ingredients loosely into the appropriate cup. Do not tap the cup on a bench or tightly pack the ingredients unless directed to do so. Level top of measuring cups and measuring spoons with a knife. When measuring liquids, place a clear glass or plastic jug with metric markings on a flat surface to check accuracy at eye level.

Note: North America, NZ and the UK use 15ml tablespoons. All cup and spoon measurements are level.

We use large eggs having an average weight of 60g.

OVEN TEMPERATURES

These oven temperatures are only a guide for conventional ovens.
For fan-forced ovens, check the manufacturer's manual.

	°C (CELSIUS)	°F (FAHRENHEIT)	GAS MARK
Very slow	120	250	½
Slow	150	275-300	1-2
Moderately slow	160	325	3
Moderate	180	350-375	4-5
Moderately hot	200	400	6
Hot	220	425-450	7-8
Very hot	240	475	9

ARE YOU MISSING SOME OF THE WORLD'S FAVOURITE COOKBOOKS?

The Australian Women's Weekly Cookbooks are available from bookshops, cookshops, supermarkets and other stores all over the world. You can also buy direct from the publisher, using the order form below.

TITLE	RRP	QTY
Almost Vegetarian	£5.99	
Asian Meals in Minutes	£5.99	
Babies & Toddlers Good Food	£5.99	
Barbecue Meals In Minutes	£5.99	
Basic Cooking Class	£5.99	
Beginners Cooking Class	£5.99	
Beginners Simple Meals	£5.99	
Beginners Thai	£5.99	
Best Ever Slimmers' Recipes	£5.99	
Best Food	£5.99	
Best Food Desserts	£5.99	
Best Food Fast	£5.99	
Best Food Mains	£5.99	
Cakes Cooking Class	£5.99	
Caribbean Cooking	£5.99	
Casseroles	£5.99	
Chicken Meals in Minutes	£5.99	
Chinese Cooking Class	£5.99	
Christmas Cooking	£5.99	
Cocktails	£5.99	
Cooking for Friends	£5.99	
Creative Cooking on a Budget	£5.99	
Detox	£5.99	
Dinner Beef	£5.99	
Dinner Lamb	£5.99	
Dinner Seafood	£5.99	
Easy Australian Style	£5.99	
Easy Curry	£5.99	
Easy Spanish-Style	£5.99	
Essential Soup	£5.99	
Freezer, Meals from the	£5.99	
French Cooking Class	£5.99	
French Food, New	£5.99	
Fresh Food for Babies & Toddlers	£5.99	
Get Real, Make a Meal	£5.99	

TITLE	RRP	QTY
Good Food Fast	£5.99	
Great Lamb Cookbook	£5.99	
Greek Cooking Class	£5.99	
Healthy Heart Cookbook	£5.99	
Indian Cooking Class	£5.99	
Japanese Cooking Class	£5.99	
Kids' Birthday Cakes	£5.99	
Kids Cooking	£5.99	
Lean Food	£5.99	
Low-carb, Low-fat	£5.99	
Low-fat Feasts	£5.99	
Low-fat Food For Life	£5.99	
Low-fat Meals in Minutes	£5.99	
Main Course Salads	£5.99	
Middle Eastern Cooking Class	£5.99	
Midweek Meals in Minutes	£5.99	
Muffins, Scones & Bread	£5.99	
New Casseroles	£5.99	
New Classics	£5.99	
New Finger Food	£5.99	
Party Food and Drink (Oct 05)	£5.99	
Pasta Meals in Minutes	£5.99	
Potatoes	£5.99	
Quick Meals in Minutes	£5.99	
Salads: Simple, Fast & Fresh	£5.99	
Saucery	£5.99	
Sensational Stir-Fries	£5.99	
Short-order Cook	£5.99	
Slim	£5.99	
Sweet Old Fashioned Favourites	£5.99	
Thai Cooking Class	£5.99	
Vegetarian Meals in Minutes	£5.99	
Weekend Cook	£5.99	
Wicked Sweet Indulgences	£5.99	
Wok Meals in Minutes	£5.99	
TOTAL COST:	**£**	

NAME

ADDRESS

POSTCODE

DAYTIME PHONE

I ENCLOSE MY CHEQUE/MONEY ORDER FOR £

OR PLEASE CHARGE MY VISA, ACCESS OR MASTERCARD NUMBER

CARD HOLDER'S NAME

EXPIRY DATE

CARDHOLDER'S SIGNATURE

To order: Mail or fax – photocopy or complete the order form above, and send your credit card details or cheque payable to: Australian Consolidated Press (UK), Moulton Park Business Centre, Red House Road, Moulton Park, Northampton NN3 6AQ, phone (+44) (0) 1604 497531, fax (+44) (0) 1604 497533, e-mail books@acpuk.com Or order online at www.acpuk.com

Non-UK residents: We accept the credit cards listed on the coupon, or cheques, drafts or International Money Orders payable in sterling and drawn on a UK bank. Credit card charges are at the exchange rate current at the time of payment.

Postage and packing UK: Add £1.00 per order plus 50p per book.

Postage and packing overseas: Add £2.00 per order plus £1.00 per book.

Offer ends 31.12.2006

Test Kitchen
Food director *Pamela Clark*
Food editor *Karen Hammial*
Assistant food editor *Amira Georgy*
Test Kitchen manager *Cathie Lonnie*
Home economists *Nancy Duran, Benjamin Haslam, Nicole Jennings, Elizabeth Macri, Christina Martignago, Sharon Reeve, Susie Riggall, Kirrily Smith*
Editorial coordinator *Rebecca Steyns*

The Australian Women's Weekly
Food director *Lyndey Milan*
Food editor *Alexandra McCowan*
Deputy food editor *Frances Abdallaoui*
Photographers: *Alan Benson, Joe Filshie, Mark O'Mera, Brett Stevens, Stuart Scott*
Stylists: *Sopha Young, Georgina Doling, Marie-Helene Clauzon, Carolyn Fienbery, Amber Keller, Katy Holder*

ACP Books
Editorial director *Susan Tomnay*
Creative director *Hieu Chi Nguyen*
Senior editor *Wendy Bryant*
Designer *Rachel Black*
Sales director *Brian Cearnes*
Marketing director *Matt Dominello*
Brand manager *Renée Crea*
Production manager *Carol Currie*
Chief executive officer *John Alexander*
Group publisher *Pat Ingram*
Publisher *Sue Wannan*
Editorial director (AWW) *Deborah Thomas*
Produced by ACP Books, Sydney.
Printed by Dai Nippon Printing in Korea.
Published by ACP Publishing Pty Limited, 54 Park St, Sydney; GPO Box 4088, Sydney, NSW 2001.
Ph: (02) 9282 8618 Fax: (02) 9267 9438.
acpbooks@acp.com.au
www.acpbooks.com.au
To order books, phone 136 116.
Send recipe enquiries to: recipeenquiries@acp.com.au
RIGHTS ENQUIRIES
Laura Bamford, Director ACP Books.
lbamford@acplon.co.uk
Ph: +44 (207) 812 6526
AUSTRALIA: Distributed by Network Services, GPO Box 4088, Sydney, NSW 2001.
Ph: (02) 9282 8777 Fax: (02) 9264 3278.
UNITED KINGDOM: Distributed by Australian Consolidated Press (UK), Moulton Park Business Centre, Red House Rd, Moulton Park, Northampton, NN3 6AQ.
Ph: (01604) 497531 Fax: (01604) 497533
acpukltd@aol.com
CANADA: Distributed by Whitecap Books Ltd, 351 Lynn Ave, North Vancouver, BC, V7J 2C4.
Ph: (604) 980 9852 Fax: (604) 980 8197
customerservice@whitecap.ca
www.whitecap.ca
NEW ZEALAND: Distributed by Netlink Distribution Company, ACP Media Centre, Cnr Fanshawe and Beaumont Streets, Westhaven, Auckland.
PO Box 47906, Ponsonby, Auckland, NZ.
Ph: (09) 366 9966 ask@ndcnz.co.nz
SOUTH AFRICA: Distributed by PSD Promotic, 30 Diesel Road Isando, Gauteng Johannesbu PO Box 1175, Isando 1600, Gauteng Johanne
Ph: (2711) 392 6065 Fax: (2711) 392 6079
orders@psdprom.co.za

Clark, Pamela.
The Australian Women's Weekly
Best Food Fast

Includes index.
ISBN 1 86396 406 1

1. Quick and easy cookery. I. Title: Best Food
II. Title: Australian Women's Weekly

641.555

© ACP Publishing Pty Limited 2005
ABN 18 053 273 546

First published 2005. Reprinted 2005 (twice).

The publishers would like to thank the followin for props used in photography:
Mud; Accoutrement; Plenty; Wheel and Barre